WHAT IS OCCULTISM?
Its Secrets and Its Reasons

by
PAPUS

PAPUS
DOCTOR GERARD ENCAUSSE

WHAT IS OCCULTISM?

Psychology - Metaphysics - Logic - Morals - Theodicy
- Sociology - Practices - Traditions of Occultism

1892

Translated by
Sâr Phosphoros

Sovereign Grand Commander
Christian Knights of Saint-Martin

HAINESVILLE, IL

What is Occultism? Its Secret and Its Reason (1892)
by Papus

Translated by Sâr Phosphoros

First English Edition
Published January 2022
Copyright ©2017, 2022 Sâr Phosphoros
All rights reserved.

ISBN: 978-1-946814-02-9

Triad Press, LLC
260 E. Belvidere Rd. #357
Hainesville, IL 60030

Table of Contents

INTRODUCTION vii
WHAT IS OCCULTISM? 1
THEORY 4
METAPHYSICS 14
LOGIC 18
MORALS 23
AESTHETICS 26
THEODICY[7] 30
SOCIOLOGY 34
THE PRACTICE OF OCCULTISM OR MAGIC 36
TRADITION 53
INFLUENCES OF THE OCCULT SOCIETIES 63
CONCLUSION 75
ENDNOTES 77

INTRODUCTION

It seems, from the very first, that a little courage of the hopeless is necessary in order to even speak on spiritualist philosophy in our era of positive science and at a moment when psycho-physiology seems to have to embrace into its domain of experience all or nearly all that belonged up till now to classical philosophy.

What gives us this courage is that we ourselves have passed through this phase of materialist positivism and we have come out of it, as will come out of it, in our opinion, all those who will find in science itself the responses to the first objections raised by the scientific studies against vague metaphysics and the affirmations without proof which constitute the classical spiritualist philosophy of Cousin and his successors.

The path which has led us to our present conceptions concerning Man, the Universe, and God, is far from being new, since it is attached to those ideas taught in the temples of Egypt since 2600 BC, and which have later constituted Platonism and, in a large part, Neoplatonism.

Now, before the difficulties experienced by materialist positivism to give an explanation of the psychological phenomena which multiply at the present hour, like those connected to intuition, telepathy, prophetic dreams, and the transformation of matter under the influence of that force emanated from man and called psychic, before these difficulties, the seekers of good faith have come to ask of it something other than insults, negations, or evocations of coincidence or hallucination which hide an artful spite.

Many of these seekers have addressed themselves to that ancient philosophy of the Patriarchs of the Egyptian initiators of Moses, of the Gnostics and Christian Illuminati, of the Alchemists, and of the Rose-Croix, which has never varied in its teachings across the ages and which explains today as easily the matters of spiritism and deep hypnosis as it explained at the time of the eighteenth Egyptian dynasty the connections between the Kha and the Khu, of the physical body and the luminous body in their action on the Bai, on the intelligent Spirit. This philosophy is presently known under the name of Occultism, and it is its manner of viewing spiritualism that we are to summarize to our best in the following pages.

But one thing frightens us: this is a treatise, or rather an exposé of philosophy that we are led to make, and we are a rather poor philosopher, as the prudent critics will not fail to note.

The studies of medicine, such as they are understood at the present time, make up rare clinical physicians, vague anatomists, some physiologists, but not philosophers in the elevated sense of this word.

We will not speak of the public schools which see to give the bachelor aspirants some months of the history of the motley philosophy of infantile metaphysics; like everything that the public schools do, it is necessary to do it again later, if one wishes to draw from it any real profit.

There remains the theological studies, the seminaries, and the higher lay studies of the Sorbonne and of the College de France. The pupils of Saint Thomas and those of Renan.

It is between them and the physiologists that give

themselves to the combat of contemporary thought. We have not, for our part, to favor one side more than the other.

Counter to many creators of philosophical systems, who begin their treatise by the systematic demolition of the systems of their predecessors and by the assertion that they bring at last the integral truth (until they suffer the fate of said predecessors), we come to declare first of all that we have created nothing original, and that our role consists in short of adapting to our epoch, a very ancient philosophy.

If our feeble pen sometimes divulges the Wisdom that it is charged to convey, we pray the seekers to refer to the originals, and to attribute the errors only to our ignorance and to our lack of eloquence. It is this guarantee which, alone, gives us the courage to lead to the end a task which appears to us above our abilities.

If the few following pages push certain minds to read more closely the masters of whom we are but a dim disciple, if the serious seekers realize that occultism is better than that collection of vague ideas under which its adversaries seek to crush it, if, finally, they press the unity that this inspiring philosophy, through the initiatic centers, of Spinoza, of Goethe, of Leibnitz, and of so many others, brings into the quarrel between Science and Belief, then our modest essay will have largely attained more than its aim.

WHAT IS OCCULTISM?

Occultism is the collection of theories, practices, and Paths of realization derived from the Occult Science.

It presents itself across the ages, as a rather distinct whole, having its theories, its methods, and up to its processes of diffusion and personal teachings. From here is the difficulty of knowing well this doctrine for those who have not penetrated into the centers where it is taught, and the numerous errors committed by the critics who have judged it without understanding it.

Before laying out Occultism in its details, let us quickly establish what differentiates it from the other philosophical systems. The theory is contained in the various sections of the Occult Science that we are henceforth obliged to define in order to avoid the confusions with the Divinatory Arts that we sometimes call "occult sciences."

1. While Science, such as it is understood by the contemporary scholars, studies above all the physical phenomena and the accessible and visible part of Nature and Man, the Occult Science, thanks to its preferred method: Analogy, strives in departing from the physical matters, to rise to the study of the invisible, occult part of Nature and Man; from here is its first characteristic of "Science of the Hidden," Scientia Occultati.

2. While contemporary Science diffuses, through journals and public experiments, its discoveries and practices, the Occult Science divides its research into two categories:

A. One part which may be published in order to aid

in the progress of humanity.

B. A part which must be reserved to a selection of men; from here is the second character of this Hidden Science: Scientia Occulta.

3. Finally, while intellectual proofs alone are required of the candidates by the faculties and great contemporary scientific schools, the centers of occultist teaching require, moreover, various moral proofs, and confide their teachings only to men proven capable of never employing for evil the knowledge that they have been able to acquire. Thus, all the books and all the publications relating to the reserved subjects are written according to a special symbolic method, which shows us again the Occult Science under the new aspect of Scientia Occultans.

Such is the theoretical base upon which Occultism is supported, the ancient as much as the contemporary. We have no judgment to bear on these various points, having to limit ourselves to the exposition from obscurity of a subject too beloved to not exact our full attention.

Occultism is indeed, then, the representative of a sort of special scientific Society, distinct from the Universities, and, as there have always existed men preferring its methods to those of the current Science, and as it possesses a particular literature and affects a supreme contempt for the exclusively material methods of investigation, and as, finally, there still exist in our day and in nearly every land, occult fraternities of initiation, it seems to us indispensable to analyze this system:

      1st, from the philosophical point of view;

      2nd, from the historical point of view;

      3rd, from the point of view of its special paths of

diffusion and realization in the various eras. Moreover, we have to make a necessary distinction between the theoretical part and the practical or experiential part, generally known under the name of "Magic."

THEORY

Occultism From the Philosophical Point of View

Occultism, being a complete philosophical system, ought to be studied in its teachings concerning: *Psychology, Metaphysics, Logic, Morals, Aesthetics, Theodicy, Sociology*, and various other theoretical applications, that we will analyze successively and in that order, before occupying ourselves with the history.

Union of the Soul and the Body - Constitution of Man - Feminine Principle

From the psychological point of view, the first and most important problem which presents itself is that of the connections of the spiritual principle with the material principle, or the means of union of the soul with the body.

This brings us to the definition of the constitution of man, such as the occultists understand it, and on which they have never varied their teachings in any era, so much that the Egyptians of the fifteenth dynasty described the properties and characteristics of the "Ka" or Luminous Double exactly as Paracelsus described this "astral body" in the 16th century of our era, and as Eliphas Lévi studied the "Fluidic Double" in 1863. For the occultists, man is constituted by three principles, tonalized into one general unity. These principles are:

1. The Physical Body, considered only as the product and the support of the other elements;

2. The Astral Body, doubly polarized, and which unites the inferior, physical to the superior, spiritual;

3. The Immortal Spirit.

Of these various elements, one alone is particular to the occultists; it is the second, or astral body, the other two being studied with care, the first by the anatomists and physiologists, the third by the psychologists and philosophers. This constitution of man in three Principles is so characteristic of traditional Occultism that it suffices to determine its representative in every era, and it permits to distinguish, within Occultism itself, the truly traditional schools from the plagiarists or the awkward compilations made in various eras under the cover of the occult. Concerning the human being, the teaching may be summarized in these propositions:

1. Man is constituted by three principles, synthesized into one Unity, or doctrine of the Tri-Unity.

2. Man is analogous (but not similar) to the Universe, or doctrine of the Microcosm or Lesser World (Man) and the Macrocosm or Greater World (the Universe).

3. There is a strict correspondence between each element of Man and his analogue in the Universe. This is the doctrine of correspondences, upon which Magic is based, and on which we will speak again with respect to its practice.

In all this, what interests us for the moment is the astral body, that Plastic Mediator that the classical philosophers have condemned, often without taking the trouble to study it attentively, and which reappears in every epoch sometimes under different names, but with characteristics identical in the works of the occultists. To know well the astral body is to possess the most important of the keys of the doctrine which occupies us; let us stop then for a moment on the reasons given by the occultists to support their assertions. The use of the analogy allows one to make use of comparisons, not in order to demonstrate, but to clarify a question.

Let us begin, then, by establishing a comparison intended to project some light on the subject.

Man is compared to a vehicle whose carriage represents the physical body, the horse, the astral body, and the coachman, the spirit. This image allows one to grasp well the role of each principle.

The carriage is inert by itself and corresponds well to the physical body, such as the occultists understands it. The Coachman commands the direction by the reins, without participating in the direct pulling; this is the role of the Spirit. Finally, the Horse, united by the shafts to the carriage and by the reins to the Coachman, moves the whole system, without occupying itself with direction.

This image indicates to us well the character of the astral body; true horse of the organism, which moves but does not direct. It remains to us to see whether this comparison corresponds to a real entity, and whether there really exists in us a motor Principle, distinct from the directing Principle. It is to physiology and anatomy that the contemporary occultists have addressed themselves in order to prove the assertion of their ancestors on this subject.[1]

There exists in us a nervous system of organic life, placed under the cup nearly exclusive of the Grand Sympathetic nerve and acting on organs with a special

What is Occultism?

constitution (organs with smooth fibers). This system moves everything in the organism, from the finest of arteries, to the intestine during sleep.

In the state of wakefulness, the muscles with striated fibers add to this action that of the Brain, seat of the Spirit, and thus the Coachman of the organism comes to demonstrate that its role is quite distinct from that of the horse which represents the Grand Sympathetic, served by its plexuses and its multiple vasomotor nerves.

While we sleep, the cerebral functions cease, and only the system of organic life pursues its action: it digests the food, fabricates the chyle and lymph; it circulates the blood and distributes everywhere Force and Matter; it does even more, for it is that which presides over the defense of the Organism by throwing the leucocytes at the point of attack, and by re-closing the small wounds made by carelessness or accident. Now, that is indeed the principle that Paracelsus called "the Hidden Worker"; its domain is quite separated from that of the Spirit, which has other things to do than to preside over the pleasantries of chylification and excretion. Such are the teachings of the occultists concerning the relationship of the astral body with the physical body; let us see what they say in order to explain its relationship with the Spirit.

The astral body, being the house keeper in the human being, presides over the elaboration of all the organic forces. Among these, one interests us from the point of view of the cerebral actions: it is the nervous force. The force which circulates in the nerves has been studied from the point of view of its rapidity, and clearly differentiated from the electricity and the other physical forces. Like all the organic fabrications, it is drawn from the blood, as shown by the cerebral troubles caused either by anemia or hyperthermia, and here again, the astral body presides over this elaboration. The nervous force acts with respect to the Spirit as electricity acts with respect to the telegraphist, the material brain representing the telegraph.

The occultists refute the arguments of the materialists by asserting that these latter have confused the telegraphist and the nervous force, or Spirit, with its sole means of communication with the organism. Remove the electricity from the telegraphist and this latter will seem not to exist for his correspondent, for he will be incapable of sending the least communication. It is thus that in normal or induced sleep, in grave illnesses, in fainting fits, there is a displacement of the nervous force, or a cessation of the customary production, and, for want of its indispensable means of action, the Spirit is as incapable of manifesting its presence as the Employee to send a message without electricity. We have chosen some examples taken from the contemporary sciences in order to set forth the doctrines of Occultism in a clear manner, by avoiding the references to a multitude of old technical terms which would have only served to confuse our exposé. We see now that the Plastic Mediator is something other than pure philosophical conception, and that this idea seems to correspond to a physiological reality. Let us pursue our analysis of the astral body. It is now that we are going to appeal to some experimenters who, in these later years, have wished to get a clear idea in a positive manner of the possibilities of control that these ancient, and always identical teachings presented.

The occultists claim, indeed, that the nervous system of the organic life is only the temporary support of the Principle constituting the Plastic Mediator, and that this Principle is luminous, when it is seen independently of the material organs, which is to say that this Principle can radiate around the body, in which it is normally contained.[2]

This "coming out of the astral body," according to the technical expression, may be incomplete, that is to say partial or total. In the first case, we are witness to certain phenomena studied by the Magnetizers and the Spiritists; we will speak again concerning its practice. In the second, the dividing in two of the individual may be verified at a distance by several witnesses; it is the case with several Saints of Christianity. It is in this way that the occultists explain the majority of the feats called "telepathic" and the spiritist phenomena of materialization in the majority of serious experiments, and not due to fraud.

Several contemporary seekers have wished to verify these assertions experimentally and by recording the phenomena produced on photographic plates or by means of purely mechanical apparatus, to avoid hallucinations.

The research of this kind has been summarized in the two works of one of the experimenters, Mr. A. de Rochas. An initial series of attempts has concerned the exteriorization of the senses, and the results have been clear, confirming the occult theories on the radiating of the astral body.

The second series, carried out in large part by means of a special subject: Eusapia Paladino, in the presence of numerous and impartial seekers, has concerned the study of the movement of objects at a distance and without contact, and has confirmed again the strict relation of the nervous force of the medium and the effects produced under the name of "exteriorization of the

Motot-force." These attempts are too recent, and have not yet been controlled by enough experimenters to take rank among the classical Science, any more than the research of Dr. Baraduc and Messrs. Luys and David or of Mr. Varkievitz Iodko on the photographic recording of the effluvia, combatted moreover by Dr. Guebhard. There is simply here a tendency to confirm the occultist theories by the processes of contemporary science and by experimenters who are by no means occultists, who deserved to be indicated at this place. This astral body has, therefore, the different following roles, according to Occultism:

1. It unites, by a double polarization, the physical body to the Spirit;

2. It is the hidden worker accomplishing the functions of vegetative life and preserving the material body, which it maintains and repairs unceasingly, its form, despite the continual death of the physical cells, and its functional harmony despite illness and imprudence;

3. Finally, it can radiate around the individual, forming a sort of invisible atmosphere called the "Astral Aura" and it can even exteriorize itself totally. It is thanks to these various properties of the astral body that the occultists give an account of the visions and actions at a distance, presentiments, prophetic ecstasy, dreams of madness, and other phenomena classified by the philosophers into special psychology and in the chapter of coincidences or hallucinations.

We cannot leave Psychology without saying a word on the doctrines of Occultism concerning the feminine principle, in the various planes and especially in the human plane. The feminine, for the occultist, is the necessary complement of the active principle. The Woman is therefore neither superior nor inferior to the Man; she is complementary, psychologically as well as anatomically. The Woman is the materialization, in Humanity, of the universal plastic faculty, symbolized by the Dove. She develops and perfects the forms created by the Man: that is why she must develop her animic faculties, whereas the Man must focus on the development of his intellectual faculties. To seek to demonstrate that the woman is inferior or superior to the man, is to seek whether the zinc pole is superior, because it is active, to the carbon pole, which remains passive in the battery. They are both indispensable to the production of the current, and if they depart from their respective role, the current no longer passes. This double polarity exists, not only in the different sexes, but also within each individual. The heart is always complementary to the brain, and, therefore, it is positive with the woman and negative with the man.

By "heart," it must be understood the sentiments and the animic faculties that the occultists localize in the cardiac Plexus, as point of origin, the brain serving only, in this case, as center of reflection. For the Tri-Unity being an absolutely general law, each of the three organic centers of man: the Abdomen, the Chest, and the Head, has its very personal anatomical, physiological, and psychological functions.[3]

The sensations are localized in the solar plexus and constitute, with the lower bulge of the Medulla, the center of psychological localization of the abdomen. The cardiac plexus forms with the thoracic bulge of the medulla, the center of localization of the sentiments, and finally, the sympathetic plexus or the head constitutes the animal intellect which forms our lower unconscious.

These three lower psychological centers, that Plato has described and of which they have made three souls, are governed and led in the unity of Consciousness by the immortal Spirit, charged with controlling and directing the sensitive, passionate, or intellectual impulses which assail various organic centers. It is from the more or less intense action of the Reason and the will upon these various impulses that arises the greater or lesser force of free will in each of us and personal responsibility.

Man, being the Microcosm, contains, analogically within him, all the psychologies of the lower kingdoms, represented by his three sections: the abdomen corresponding to the mineral kingdom, the chest to the vegetable kingdom, and the head to the animal kingdom. Reciprocally, each animal is but the materialization of the psychological impulse which will be found in man. The Tiger, the Ox, the Ant, the Bee, the Pig are but living symbols, each, of a faculty of organic man. The use of these correspondences gives the key, not only of the magical rites, but also of the aesthetic derived from the teachings of the occultist tradition. The souls of the animals are the result of an evolution, and they will evolve still until they have attained to the animal part of man, whereas the immortal Spirit is the result of a descent, of an "involution" as the occultists say. It is in reference to this teaching that an ancient has said: "The souls of animals come from the terrestrial fire (symbolic figure of the evolutionary current) whereas the human souls come from the heavens."

We have intentionally dwelled upon psychology;

we are going to approach the other sections of the occult philosophy more rapidly.

METAPHYSICS

The Astral Plane - The Astral Stereotypes – Evolution

If psychology offered us, in the problem of the union of the soul and body, the occasion to specify the rather special theories of occultism on this subject, *Metaphysics* is going to show us, furthermore, personal applications of the occult philosophy to the solution of the most important of the problems of metaphysic: the passage of the Being to Reality, or from the Subjective to the Objective. When the occultists have asserted that the solution to this kind of problem resides in the existence of a doubly polarized intermediary, it is claimed that they have deferred the difficulty instead of resolving it.

However, the Astral Body is an organic reality and not a philosophical concept; it is the same for the "astral plane" or intermediary plane between the Being and physical Reality, thanks to which the occultists claims to resolve this important problem.

In order to give an initial idea of the functioning of this astral plane, let us borrow again from one of our scientific contemporaries, the photograph, some necessary examples. Theoretically, the passing of the object to produce the proof or photographic image of this object, would be made directly and without intermediary. A philosopher of the classical school would not fail to say that this intermediary is a useless invention, and he could cite the example of the painter or sketch artist who reproduces the object directly on linen or paper, without having need of any intermediary. However, the photograph first obtains a negative stereotype, that is to say where all the tints are the inverse of physical nature, and it is by an inversion of the first result undergoing an operation by the light itself that it has provided for the artist to obtain the positive proof, similar to the model.

This stereotype plate which, theoretically, could be considered as useless, plays, on the contrary, a very important role since it allows one to obtain an indefinite series of positive images. Now, the astral plane is for the occultist but the plane of the negative "stereotype plates" or molds from which all the physical objects are but proofs, each drawn from a more or less large number of exemplars, by special spiritual agents. The passage from the subjective to the objective is thus justified.

And this doctrine of intermediaries plays such a role in occultism that we will find it in connection with the question of the origin of the Idea.

Thought is considered, in the occult tradition, as one of the most powerful and most effective forces in action in the universe. The ideas are active agents of good fortune or misfortune according to the character of their center of emission and according to the intensity of this emission. The question of their first origin, an entirely metaphysical question, is settled by Claude de Saint-Martin, the great occult philosopher, by showing that the germ alone of the ideas is innate in us, as the oak is only in germ in the acorn. The sensation comes to be developed and makes to fructify certain of these germs of ideas, as the heat and water develop the oak. To the materialist theory of the ideas derived solely from the sensations, occultism comes to show the common point of union by revealing the character and the mode of development of the idea-germs and their role as intermediaries between the various planes.

Thus it is rather difficult to really classify occultism into a well-defined metaphysical system.

Occultism claims, indeed, to play the role of universal conciliator between all the systems. It teaches that dualism and materialism are true, if one restricts their application to the physical plane; but that one errs if they wish to extend this application to the other planes. Likewise, Pantheism is the system which gives the best account of the life of its laws in the astral plane, just as pure spiritualism, by going even unto mysticism, may, alone, effectively give an account of the laws of the divine plane of creation.

But the occultist is forbidden from remaining exclusively in any of these planes, as much as the exclusive adoption of each of these metaphysical systems. It aims at the conciliation of the Thesis, Antithesis, and Synthesis in a strict and universal union that it calls "La Mathèse."

Idealizing Materialism and materializing Idealism, Occultism is absolutely forbidden from being a pantheist system, and if it were necessary to classify it, we would have to create a new case and catalogue it as a synthetic or integral idealism.

In antiquity, each science, even that of the numbers, had a physical section and a metaphysical section. Later, the physical section was, alone, the object of research followed by part of the classical schools, and this resulted in the marvelous conquests of experimental science, disdaining metaphysical digressions more and more. This was the domain abandoned to occultism, and it has always preserved the study of each science so that at the present time, its adepts claim that Alchemy alone contains the metaphysics of the present Chemistry, just as Astrology, alone, may give a philosophy of Astronomy, and Magic a key to the real Causes of the forces, of which Physics verifies the more material effects. So an occultist, initiated into one of the initiatic schools, regards as a vulgar profane, the one who says that Alchemy, Astrology, and Magic have been but the first and more primitive form of Chemistry, Astronomy, and Physics.

The framework of our exposé does not permit us to expound upon the Metaphysics of each science, and we are obliged to choose only from a small number of applications. In Natural History, Occultism gives some very interesting theories on the evolution and organization of the species and of individuals. For the occultist, indeed, it is the astral body which fabricates the physical body, in the uterus of the mother (for the higher species) or in the egg, according to the case. The evolution from one type to the type immediately superior, takes place then on the astral plane. The mold of the body of a dog, for example, becomes, after the sufferings of a terrestrial incarnation (or physical incarnation on any planet) the mold or astral body of a future ape body. Such is the reason which has prevented until now the experimenters from verifying on earth the direct passage from one species to another though this passage is evident, for the anatomist, as for the one who observes the evolution of the embryo. This is the descending or involutive current which comes to regulate the spiral of evolution in all the planes of the universe.

LOGIC

Analogy, the Numbers

If Occultism presents itself to us with so personal a character in these first two philosophical regards, it will be the same thereof for the third: Logic. Here again, Occultism is going to show its originality by the use of a method which is nearly exclusively personal to it: Analogy, which comes to support the deduction and induction in all the occultists works. The great difficulty for the use of this method is to not confuse analogy with similitude, and not to believe that two analogous things are forcibly similar: thus, the brain and the heart are analogous in occult, yet they are far from being similar. This holds to the doctrine of correspondences of which we have already said a word. It is the things placed in the same column of correspondence which are analogous, and the character of the analogy is determined by the general sense of the entire column.

Thus, according to the philosophical anatomy of Malfatti de Montereggio, the stomach, the heart, and the brain play the role of embryos respective to each of the three centers: abdominal, thoracic, and cephalic, in which they are contained. These organs are analogous, then, between themselves according to this function. But we may also establish their analogy according to other elements of appreciation. If we consider, indeed, these three organs from the point of view of their general fun tion, we will establish that the first receives directly from the exterior world of food, the second, from the

What is Occultism?

atmospheric air, and the third from the sensations. There is therefore analogy from the point of view of the direct reception of an external property: the food, the air, and the sensations exist equally between them, for the analogy of the two things between them determines the analogy of all the constituents of these two things. We see the considerable elasticity of this method which, under it apparent simplicity, is very difficult to handle with sagacity and precision. Thus does it seem to us indispensable, given the exceptional importance of the analogy in occultism, to establish a table, an example of use of this method applied to anatomy and elementary physiology, so as not to depart from our first examples.

Analogy is the theoretical method that the occultists reserve to their research concerning the physical plane and the World of Laws.

It allows one to have some second-hand knowledge of the world of Principles and of First Causes. In order to penetrate this Plane, the occultists advanced in the practice possess a method of direct vision into the invisible World, formerly cultivated with care in the schools of prophets, then utilized by the ecstatics and mystics, and preserved solely, in our day, by some rare adepts of the Chinese societies, Brahmanic fraternities, or by envoys of the higher planes. Here again, Occultism, which had appeared to us almost as a simple philosophical system, abruptly escapes the general method in order to appeal to the mysterious practices to which it owes its name, and also many ridiculous slanders widespread on its account by the ignorant and the sectarians. This second method has been nearly exclusively utilized for research concerning the soul and its transformations after Death, as

Logic

well as the spiritual beings which populate the various invisible planes of the Universe. Apollonius of Tyana, Jacob Bœhme, and Swedenborg are, with Claude de Saint-Martin and his Master de Pasqually, the best known of the philosophers having employed this method; which has had them classified among the mystics.

We will speak on this subject with respect to the Practice.

The union of analogy and direct vision has given birth to the use of Numbers and Symbols, such as the occultists practice it.

Indeed, to avoid the errors to which the inappropriate use of analogy could lend itself, the Kabbalah (see *Cabbale*)[4] has given a precious instrument of control in the Numbers and their symbolic conception. Each number corresponds, indeed, to an idea and to a characteristic hieroglyph, so well that the laws of the combinations of the Symbols and Ideas (see *Tarot*). One will find, in the works of the Pythagoreans, who were particularly devoted to this genre of applications, some interesting information on this subject. Plutarch has summarized some of them in his *Treatise* on *Isis* and *Osiris*. It is through this treatise that we have an idea of the triangular and lozengic [diamond-shaped] numbers acknowledged by the occultists under the same title as the square and cubic numbers. It is the same of the current arithmetical operations, to which the occultists add:

1. *Theosophical Addition*, which consists, being given any number from 1 to 9, in adding all the numbers from the Unity up to the number considered.

Here, for example:

What is Occultism?

The number 5, to have its theosophical addition, we add 1, 2, 3, 4, and 5; that is to say all the numbers from 1 to the number considered, 5.

This gives 15.

The number 4 would give, by the same process, 10.

2. *Theosophical Reduction*, which consists in reducing the numbers composed of two or more numerals, into a number of one single numeral, by the successive addition of all the numerals constituting the number, until what remains is but a single numeral.

Example: the number 25 is reduced to $2+5=7$.

The number 34,224 is reduced successively in the following manner: $3+4+2+2+4=15$

$15=1+5=6$

Therefore, $34,224=6$ in its final reduction.

Claude de Saint-Martin, in his book on the Numbers, calls the result of theosophical addition the *essential root*, and he made it the complement of the square roots and cubic roots. To conclude this brief survey on the Numbers, it remains to us to relate the meaning of those most commonly utilized, from the symbolic point of view, by the occultists.

1 - The Positive Principle.

2 - The Negative Principle.

3 - The First equilibrated term, resulting from the action of the two preceding principles.

4 - The first material form.

5 - Action of the Active Principle (1) upon the form (4), Life.

6 - The equilibrium of the forces, the two

Logic

involutive and evolutive currents of Nature, represented hieroglyphically be the Seal of Solomon. (Two triangles interlaced and with summits opposed.)

7 - Action of the equilibrating force (3) upon the form (4), first perfect term.

8 - Equilibrium of the forms. Justice.

9 - Triple ternary, symbol of the three material planes.

10 - Action of the Active Principle (1) upon the Nothingness (O). First complete creation, image and model of all the others.

We will stop here with these examples which could be considerably developed. Each number has, indeed, at least three meanings with various adaptations in the various planes. The Kabbalists have especially labored over this question. (See also *Tarot*.)[5]

MORALS

Reincarnation[6]

Morals, such as the occultists understand it, is most rigorous and most elevated. It is based for the majority of the schools, on submission to all the charges imposed, whether by the social condition or by the trials whose acceptance is as indispensable as are the consequences of later faults. Occultism teaches, indeed, that the spirit is reincarnated successively into several physical bodies, and that we pay, in the following existence, for the faults not atoned for in a previous life.

Between each incarnation, the soul is made aware of all its anterior existences and of their consequences from the point of view of its evolution.

At the beginning of each descent unto the physical plane, by contrast, the Spirit loses memory of the past, which is necessary in order to avoid suicides which would become almost inevitable for whoever would have awareness of the faults that they come to expiate. This doctrine constituted, as well as that of the Divine Unity, one of the most redoubtable mysteries of the ancient initiations, and it was taught under the veil of the Fable. The water of the river Lethe that the soul drank when coming out of the inferior places (Infera) is a reminder of this mystery. The possession of Power or wealth is considered, by the occultists, as one of the most dangerous and most difficult trials which may assault man. If the powerful or the rich, forgetting that he is but a simple depositary of the vital force of the Society, makes himself the center and places exclusively for himself and his own what has been entrusted to him, then the punishment will be all the more terrible. When a young student, deeply moved by the apparent iniquities of Destiny, came to protest to the Master against the persistent misfortune which overwhelmed such or such man, the Master evoked, for a moment, the images inscribed formerly in the secret light surrounding the individual, and the student, recognizing the man presently unhappy in this former wealth which helped none of the poor but by vanity, understood and blessed his Master. The moral teachings of Occultism have always been almost exclusively practical; they avert the pupils from suicide, not by giving them philosophical discourses on the nothingness of this act, but rather by placing them face to face in the astral plane with the spirit of one who has committed suicide, and by showing them the indescribable horrors of the dissolution of the unfortunate.

It is the same with death, all the phases of which are studied experientially. Thus the occultist, initiated after another manner than in the books, affects a singular contempt for this phenomenon of the passage from one plane to another, which he has seen realized, or, if he is advanced enough, that he has realized himself, several times, experientially. A moral based upon such practices is forcibly very powerful, especially when personal research has led the postulant to verify the exact character and truth of the greater part of the religious traditions, and especially the Christian traditions.

It is curious to ascertain that the Rose-Croix Illuminati have always shown themselves as ardent apologists of Christianity, all while maintaining the greatest

What is Occultism?

severity for the clergy whom they accuse of having delivered Christ to Caesar, by participating in the sharing of temporal power and gold. Thus has the Church, in every era, made the greatest efforts to put a stop to the occultists movement, which makes men of such faith and such independence of character, that it wishes only to see them as the agents of hell. We may summarize the rules of the occultist Moral in some propositions, the development of which will be found in the works of Eliphas Lévi: The occultist must know how to abstain, to suffer, to pray, to die, and to forgive. Once more, what interests us in this moral, is not so much these rules that we will find more or less among all moralists, as the practical path of demonstration by direct vision.

This path exists from Masters worthy of this name, and they fled the tumult and renown; they are known only by some. Those that the public takes for chiefs are, generally, those who have been delegated to the works of propaganda: they are the realizers, the men of action, the arms of the initiatic organisms. Certain ones have believed or wished to have believed that such masters existed only in the Orient; this is an error. Our information permits us to affirm that there exist, not at Paris, but in some towns of France, Masters of different degrees, who live far from the commotion and publicity, who are unknown, under their true character, even by their closest neighbors.

AESTHETICS

Symbolism - The Sphinx - The Temperaments

The Aesthetic is, perhaps, the part of philosophy in which the influence of Occultism has been most considerable. Symbolism is, indeed, one of the most developed sections of the occult, and it has guided, not only the sculptors and painters initiated into the secret tradition, but also the poets and the historians, from the greatest antiquity until the 16th century of our era. Let us point out in passing this very characteristic trait of the historians educated according to the occultist method: they never dwell upon the history of the individuals, and are only interested in the history of the Principles that incarnate said individuals. This was the exclusive method of the ancients, taken up again by the prophets; they wrote the development of the initiatic Science of all times, under the name of *Hermes*.

When the modern writers have wished to apply their current individualist process to this historical symbolism, they have been surprised in ascertaining that Hermes would have been the author of 20,000 volumes, which is much for one man alone, but which is quite normal for the central University of Egypt (of which Hermes is the collective name). It is the same of Zoroaster or for Buddha, which designate principles, incarnated in a series of men, and not single individuals.

When the contemporaries have seen their error, say the occultists, they have committed another by denying any personal existence to the individuals who had manifested the same Principles in various eras, and by attributing to collectives of men of the same time the works of Homer or those of Moses. The truth for the occultist is between these two extreme theories; it was a useful point to recall in passing. The *Illiad*, the *Aeneid*, the *Golden Age*, and the *Divine Comedy* are histories written according to the keys of Occultism and describing the mysteries of physical or astral Initiation.

All the gothic cathedrals are also symbols of stone, words of granite, as well as all the temples, ancient and modern, of India and China.

So as not to dwell any more than is reasonable upon this special point, let us give a very clear example of the application of the Occult to Aesthetics; this will help to understand the rest. We will choose the symbol of the Sphinx. The Sphinx, according to the occult tradition, was placed at a slight distance from the Pyramids and served as a secret entrance, thanks to a door situated between its paws.

If we analyze this symbol from the point of view of its form, we will ascertain that the sphinx, such as it has come from Chaldea, is composed of the following elements:

A human head, eagle's wings, lion's claws, bull's flanks, What, then, does this curious symbol signify? So that its meaning would never be lost, a symbolic history, that of Oedipus, explained the stone image. This history said that the hero had discerned the riddle of the Sphinx, and the word of this riddle was: MAN. All these signs which seem borrowed from animality: ox, lion, and eagle are, in reality, characteristics of man, and the Hermetic analogies are going to clarify the question.

Aesthetics

The OX is the symbol of the lymphatic temperament and of the material force which is in each of us. It is the key to the abdominal psychology or instincts, whose formula is: *To Keep Silent*.

The LION is the symbol of the sanguine temperament and of the animic force, courage, and anger. It is the key to the thoracic psychology, or the passions and sentiments, whose formula is: *To Dare*.

The EAGLE is the symbol of the nervous temperament and of the rash intellectual force, of enthusiasm and unbridled imagination. It is the key to the lower cerebral psychology, of the knowledge of books, whose formula, however elevated, is: *To Know*.

The HUMAN HEAD is the symbol of the bilous temperament and of the thoughtful will, of reason, which rules and which stops the instinctive impulses of the ox, the animic impulses of the lion, and the enthusiastic impulses of the Eagle, and leads all to the unity of the enlightened consciousness by the spirit. The formula of this psychology, no longer solely intellectual, but above all spiritual, is: *To Will*, in the sense of to will by loving, as indicates the Spanish: *Querer*.

The elements composing the Sphinx, led back according to the analogical keys, from the form to the corresponding idea, is summarized in a formula of moral and intellectual conduct: To Know, to Will, to Dare, to Keep Silent, which has guided the initiates of all the schools from the most remote antiquity. The Sphinx, gateway of initiation, is the petrified word of the occult science and of its mysterious tradition. And as the laws of Symbolism are universal, open the Gospels and you will notice, at the head of each of them and as symbol of each

What is Occultism?

evangelist, one of the four forms of the Sphinx. That is why there is a Christian Kabbalah, with the Apocalypse as especially symbolic. Thus, all the aesthetic manifestations utilized throughout antiquity, were immediately translatable into ideas, and this thanks to the symbolism of Occultism.

We could multiply the examples of these applications little-known today, and which, however, have served as model to the associations of builders who have erected the majority of the gothic cathedrals. All the arts have received life under the influence of Occultism, and since this influence has been neglected, the path of inspiration in the living springs has, in great part, been cut off, assert the adepts of the Occult Science.

THEODICY[7]

Origin of Evil - The Fall - The Reintegration
Proofs of the Existence of God

With *Theodicy*, we are going to approach the truly mystical side of the occult theories. The problem of Evil, of its origin and its end, of the fall and reintegration of the human soul, of the distinction of the divine attributes and of the relationships between God and Nature, have been, indeed, the nearly exclusive object of research of the great mystics of the occultist school, the best known of which are:

Jacob Bœhme, Martinès de Pasqually, Claude de Saint-Martin (the Unknown Philosopher), and, in the transcription of the ideas of Moses on this subject, Fabre d'Olivet. It is the ideas of these Masters that we are going to do our best to summarize in this section.

For the problem of Evil, it may be summed up in these few lines: the origin of Evil must be sought in the Human Being and not elsewhere.

René Wronski, in his "Messianisme" gives the greatest details on this point: the cause of Evil is the Fall, and the end of Evil will be the reintegration of Man into God, without the first losing anything of his personality. Such are the points that we are going to strive to develop.

For the occultists, Adam does not represent an individual man, but rather the collective of all men and all women, later differentiated. This Universal Man occupied all intra-, or rather inter-zodiacal space, over which he reigned as sovereign.

What is Occultism?

This occurred after the fall and the punishment of the Rebel Angel, become the animating principle of matter, which did not yet exist, as a realization, and was only in germ like the fruit in the grain or the child in the maternal egg. The imagination of Adam, that Moses called *Aisha*, incited by the Rebel Angel, presented to the Spirit of Universal Man a reasoning which has provoked nearly all the falls, not only universal, but even individual, in all eras.

According to this, reasoning which resists and which one sees immediately and materially, is more powerful than is the ideal, invisible and perceptible only by the Spirit. Adam, seduced by this idea of his imagination, imagined that by furnishing to the Principle of Matter the means to pass from the state of germ to the state of reality, he could unite the spiritual power of God with the material power, still unknown in its consequences, and that he would thus be the Master of his creator.

This idea, once conceived, was put into execution by the Free Will of Adam, and he came to give to matter, through his alliance with it, that principle of existence which he lacked. He was immediately enveloped, in all his spiritual organs, by this matter that he believed to be able to direct at his will, and the Principle of egotism, revolt, and hatred which constituted the material essence, strove to make descend unto him all the high aspirations of Adam. The Bible, translated exoterically, says, to this end, that the Adamic being was covered by an animal skin, symbolic allegory of the real history of the fall.

It is therefore by the exercise of his Free Will that the materialization of the universal man was accomplished, and, on this point, all the mystics are unanimous. God had only to intervene in order to mitigate the consequences of this catastrophe which had materialized, at the same time as Adam, all of Nature which constituted his domain and which was to participate in his rehabilitation. In order to mitigate the action of his creature, the Creator, utilizing Time and Space which were corollaries of the physical plane, created the *Differentiation* of the collective Being: each cell of Adam became an individual human being, and Aisha became the Principle of the universal life and of the plastic form: Eve.

Man, from that time, had to purify the inferior principles that he had added to his nature, through suffering, resignation to the trials, and the abandon of his Will to the hands of his Creator. The reincarnations were the principal instrument of salvation, and as all men are the cells of one same Being, the individual salvation will be complete only when the collective salvation is accomplished.

To aid in this salvation, the Divine Word came to participate in the incarnation and its consequences, and to subdue physical Death and its terrors on its own domain. We see that the occultists, in their mystical conceptions, are essentially Christians, and the Theosophists, like Jacob Bœhme and Claude de Saint-Martin, are characteristic to this point of view.

Man must work, then, not only towards his own salvation, towards his reintegration, as said Martinès, but also towards the reintegration of the other created beings. To succeed in this goal, the Mystics have formed associations, several of which yet exist in our day.

This history of the Fall and of the Reintegration, upon which we have expatiated a little, because it is characteristic and allows the reader to approach a literature generally inaccessible, is permanent and recommences, in its general lines, for each human soul. The incarnation into the physical body represents, indeed, the first fall, and the resistance or submission of the incarnate soul to the attractions pertaining to the passions of the physical plane, will destroy or constitute the second fall.

On the other points of Theodicy, Occultism attaches itself, generally, to the Kabbalistic doctrines. Thus, the constitution of God in Three Persons: Father, Son, and Holy Spirit, has been the object of important developments on the part of Guillaume Postel and Christian Kabbalists, whose works Pistorius has gathered.

The proofs of the existence of God derive, for the slightly advanced occultist, from the direct vision of the invisible plane, and for the beginner, from the absolute adherence to the words of the Master; thus, such a discussion seems useless to the initiates. God is conceived as absolutely personal and distinct from creation, in which he is present, as the Spirit of Man is present in his body: without losing anything of his Unity.

Likewise, *God is within us, and it is here, and not in a region situated above the clouds, that one must first seek him and find him.*

The divine emanations in action everywhere in Nature, determine three fundamental planes of action: the plane of Emanation, the plane of Formation, and the plane of Materialization. It suffices to know the Three Worlds of the Kabbalah, in order to get a clear idea of all these divisions.[8]

SOCIOLOGY

Society: living organism - Synarchy

Sociology - We could not conclude the philosophical exposé of Occultism without speaking of Sociology which, always, was the object of study followed in those Temples which sent legislators such as Lycurgus, Solon, Pythagoras, Numa, etc.

For all antiquity, society was considered by the occultists as a living organism. A writer who has devoted himself especially to this question: F.-Ch. Barlet, has even strictly determined this law, by showing that society is a living being having the power to create and modify its most essential organs.

The truly moral society, for the occultist, is therefore the one which most approaches the trinitary constitution of every superior organism, and which includes a social head, thorax, and abdomen.

The Political Economy is the representation of the social abdomen, the judicial and military forces represent the thoracic double polarization, and the universities and religions, the intellectual part of society. A modern state, organized according to this concept, called Synarchy by Saint-Yves d'Alveydre, would have three chambers: an economic chamber, delegated by the syndicates, a judicial chamber, and a university and religious chamber. Suffrage is strictly professional, each voting according to his social situation in one of the three planes.

This organization has the merit of not being a purely theoretical concept, since it has functioned for several centuries and that it, alone, has lasted longer than all the later forms together. Saint-Yves d'Alveydre has dedicated to this demonstration an immense erudition and a very real talent in his Missions.

We have concluded the exposé of this theory, so full that it would require an even more considerable framework, and we are now going to tackle the part concerning the application or practice of these various theories.

THE PRACTICE OF OCCULTISM OR MAGIC

The practice of magic - Regimen - Breathing exercises - The Principles after Death - Evocation of the Dead - The sister soul - The Spirits in Nature - Sorcery and Spells - Theurgy

Just as the occultist exacts from his pupils mental aptitudes beyond intellectual knowledge, he also subjects his disciples to a particular training, bearing on the alimentary regimen and breathing, and intended to assure the control of the will over the organism, on all its planes. It is only after this preliminary training that the occultist becomes aware of the latent forces contained in nature and in man, and not yet discovered by ordinary science, though it draws nearer every day, and he can understand all which is hidden, of truths or errors, under this term of Magic.

Before, therefore, approaching the various Magics: human, natural, infernal, divine, we are going to occupy ourselves with this training and its results.

The most elevated product generated by the human organism, in its purely mechanical part, is the nervous force, and all the activity of the beginner is going to be dedicated to obtaining this nervous force, as pure and as delicate as possible, then to concentrating this force, thus purified, as quickly as he can upon a very limited point of the organism, the brain, or even the exterior, for it may be projected at a distance. Now, the production of this nervous force is directly tied to the alimentary regimen, and its purification to the very purity of this regimen, supported by suitable breathing exercises.

The diet most proper to acting efficaciously upon the nervous force is the one into which enters the fewest animal substances, and, to this purpose, the Pythagorean diet is most favorable. But this diet, just as the fast of many modern religions, was practiced only during certain times: forty days at the maximum, in all its strictness. Then, the student returned to the attenuated mixed diet or remained exclusively vegetarian, according to his temperament, his tastes, and according to the country that he inhabited.

The principal point was to avoid the introduction into the organism of what Descartes called "the Animal Spirits."

Also, all the animals having to serve as the nourishment of the priests were slaughtered according to a special rite, and not assassinated, as in our days. The excitants were absolutely proscribed; only the frankincense, the myrrh, and some plants acting directly upon the spirit were utilized.

The breathing exercises had for their aim to increase or diminish at will the quantity of carbonic acid in the blood, and this by delaying or accelerating the exhaling. Several Buddhist sects and some fraternities of Islam also practice breathing exercises. Through this training, the student entered more intimately into relations with the invisible nature, the world of dreams opened first to him, then the direct vision and intuition developed progressively, and the first steps were established on the path of the mysteries. Let us now approach the various Magics.

The Practice of Occultism or Magic

Human Magic, or that of the microcosm, contains all the direct actions of human beings over one another, and especially the action of the trained man over the untrained man. Its key is the utilization of the astral body (see: Theory) and its conscious direction, which immediately differentiates it from mediumship.

It is here that the progressive training by diet and breathing play a capital role. The practice to attain consists, in effect, in obtaining the conscious and progressive exiting of the "astral double" outside of the physical body.

This doubling, this exteriorization, as would say the modern experimenters, forms one of the most interesting applications for the spectators, but the least actually utilized, of the true practices of the high science. The beginners and the ignorant alone may believe that the doubling is anything other than a practice of psychic gymnastics. This doubling of the human being, known from the greatest antiquity, begins to be presented to contemporary experimenters, yet disguised under the feats of Telepathy, Spiritist Mediumship, and Deep Hypnosis. All these feats are tied to the coming out, not consciously, but unconsciously, of the astral body, and this latter is obtained even more easily than the first. In this kind of experiment, the subject is put to sleep, either by an assistant or under some other influence, and he produces the displacement of objects at a distance without contact and in well controlled conditions. Occultism maintains that it is not a question here of the actions of Spirits (which the majority of spiritists claim) but only an action at a distance of the astral body of the medium. The controlled experiments pursued by Mr. de Rochas and others in France and England have come to confirm in all points the

What is Occultism?

traditional assertions of Occultism by showing that there existed a direct relation between the muscle movements of the mediums and the actions produced at a distance and without fraud.

Another series of phenomena, due to the exiting of the astral body, are the feats of vision at a distance, obtained consciously by Saint Anthony of Padua, by Swedenborg, earlier still by Apollonius of Tyana, and unconsciously by some good "subjects" of the magnetizers at the beginning of the century.

It is by this process of direct vision that are controlled the assertions of the various religious revelations concerning the state and transformations of the Spirit after physical death. In this case, the occultists bringing other elements of demonstration than the philosophical reasonings, it will be useful for us to remain a bit on this point.

The SPIRIT after physical death, according to the revelations of direct vision.

Of the three elements of which the incarnate man is composed, the first, the corpse, returns to the earth or to some other modality of the physical plane, which has given the elements for an existence to the Spirit;

- the second, the astral body, is decomposed into two parts: the one, inferior, which spreads itself into the universal life and helps to decompose, in case of need, the corpse; the other, superior, becomes what Pythagoras called "the Chariot of the Soul" and envelops the Spirit in its astral evolution;

- the third, the Spirit, is alone destined to exist with the integrity of its consciousness.

It is the latter which demands, on the whole, the

most sustained interest. The occultist theory on this subject has not changed since ancient Egypt, and it is still the history of the "Voyage of the Soul" from the Book of the Dead, but understood in its true symbolism, that will be related to us by the occultists of the 18th century, of our era and even that of the 20th, calling all to the direct Vision to support their statements.

Let us summarize, then, in detail the departure of the Spirit, and let us begin at the moment of agony. At this instant, the bond between the physical body and the Spirit has just been cut, as in a fainting fit, and the astral body tends to divide itself into two parts: an inferior which remains on the physical plane, and a superior, which will evolve unto the superior astral plane. This struggle is manifested exteriorly, in the normal cases, by agony. The amount of astral which will accompany the Spirit depends, rightly, on the elevated aspirations of the human being during incarnation; and at the moment of the departure, the Spirit seeks to draw on its part as much "astrality" as possible.

It is aided in this task by the "Ancestors," the term under which is contained all the invisible beings who come to assist the soul at its departure; for the terrestrial death is, reciprocally, the astral birth. The ancestors are there in order to receive the soul which returns to them, as the parents are here in order to receive the child which is born to the earth. Before going further, let us recall that we use the expression of planes in order to indicate well that it is not a question of determined places, for Time and Space disappear at the astral plane, and everything here is, at once, in the same plane.[9]

Let us return to the Spirit. The agony has just

What is Occultism?

come to an end, each physical cell, up to here totaled up by the preponderant action of the astral body, resumes its autonomy, the decomposition of the corpse begins, and each of the little cellular beings which constituted it goes towards its special affinities. For its part, the Spirit goes through a period of trouble, during which the consciousness seeks with difficulty to do without the disappeared physical organs. This state of trouble lasts more or less for a long time, according to the aid furnished, from this side and from the other, to the Spirit for its evolution. Finally, it comes out of its nightmare, and realizes that it is actually more living than upon earth, that new organs, signs of faculties also new, are born, and that the physical communication with the material plane rapidly becomes more and more difficult; the sentiment alone serve as links between the two planes.

But the Spirit realizes that it is not yet in its true center, and it is going to stretch its best towards the second death, the death on the astral plane, which will accelerate its evolution. It depends on the moral elevation of the Spirit; it must sustain true struggles with the beings of the astral plane which wish to tear away its lower astrality. Progressively, the stripping away is done; the Glorious Body comes, atom by atom, to replace the higher astral body, and the evolution towards the divine plane is pursued. This whole path is streaked with various judgments, trials, and interrogations that Valentinus has summarized very well in his "Pistis Sophia" (translated by Amélineau). We enter then, into the cycle of the Book of the Dead, and we may stop here.

Let us recall only that a new physical incarnation will often come to accelerate a slow evolution, and let us say some words on the special cases, then that of suicides. We will occupy ourselves then with the evocation of the Spirits of the deceased.

We have taken as example the evolution of an average Spirit, for the men who, during terrestrial life have penetrated up to the second death, don to have to undergo an interruption en route, and do not return to be incarnated but on their express desire and as "Missioned," keeping the remembrance of the past and the power to converse directly with the beings of the spiritual plane. These men are the sole and legitimate masters; we recognize them by their miraculous cures and also by their humility. The certitude of the acquisition of these mysteries has greater attraction, for an elevated intelligence, than astral projection on earth or the other purely magical processes, which always hide great dangers.

But these exceptional evolutions are, in the opinion of the occultists, very rare, and the cases of fall are, on the contrary, much more frequent. Among these cases, we are going to take as example that of the *suicides* because it suffices to clarify all the others. Dante has already shown this unhappiness, suicide by love following the death of his beloved, and coming each day to the limits of Heaven to hear said: "You only go there tomorrow." Now, all the schools occupying themselves with the constitution of the invisible plane, even the more recent
not possessing any tradition, as that of the Spiritists, agree to describe identically the sufferings of those who commit suicide, which are analogous only to those of the criminals and assassins.

In awakening from the anguish, the one who has committed suicide establishes with fright that he is directly,

What is Occultism?

although invisibly, tied to the body, that he believed to have left forever. *Until the day marked for normal death*, he remains attached to this body, tortured by physical hunger and thirst, and assisting in the decomposition of the organs which, alone, would have been able to serve him and that he himself has destroyed. To these almost material sufferings are added the mental anguishes and the terrors of the incessant struggle against the larvae of the lower astral which come to claim their spoils. Directly attached to the earth that they have not left despite their thought to the contrary, these kinds of spirits possess the weak minds and the mediums, and many a case of sudden madness have no other cause, according to the occultists. When the epoch of normal death arrives, the spirit of the one who committed suicide finds his ancestors, and he is very rapidly reincarnated into a deformed body or is crippled in order to recommence the struggle that he had deserted the first time. Only those who have consciously practiced the inversive rites of Black Magic are punished with even stronger pains; those of the criminals being still less than these latter.

We mentioned the possible *evocation* of the Spirits, and some new details are indispensable to this subject. *The occultists differentiate themselves rightly from the spiritists by the difficulty with which they admit the actual communications between the living and the Spirits themselves of the deceased.*

In order to get a very clear idea of the objections raised by the occultists to this subject, it is necessary to remind oneself of the theory of the *Astral Images* on which we have spoken at length.

All terrestrial deeds are graphed, one could say photographed, in the astral light, and this rule is as true for

The Practice of Occultism or Magic

ideas as for individuals. It is in this way that a human idea is a force as dynamic and as material as heat and light; from this comes the training of the Will for the beginner. An idea leaves a trace of its activities, good or evil, in the astral plane, and this trace may be retrieved long after. It is the same for the entire individual, who leaves in the astral plane an image of his terrestrial passage. It is this image that, the majority of the time, the spiritists take for the actual apparition of the one whom they evoke. In other cases, when there is not a fraud of a medium, the actions attributed by the spiritists to the Spirits are, for the occultists, only the results of the forces emanated by the medium, and sometimes augmented by the aid of elementals.

It is no less true that when the occultists assert the reality of the communications between the two planes, and admit that a communication is even of a deceased human Spirit, they do so only by elimination and provided with all the necessary proofs. Magic claims to be able to place its adepts in a state to practice the evocation of the dead: but the rites of Necromancy are considered as very dangerous, as much for the evoker as for the spirit evoked.

One sole exceptional path permits one to be put into communication with the invisible plane, without danger: it is Theurgy. The Masters alone, generally hidden under the aspects of theurgy, have the power to act consciously upon the Spirits in all the planes of Nature, visible or invisible.

To be complete, we must mention, finally, the theory of the *sister-soul*, according to which the beings evolved upon the astral plane are formed by the fusion of two terrestrial souls which have found each other again

What is Occultism?

after ages of seeking; each of the souls preserving, moreover, the integrality of its personality. This concept lends to some charming philosophical developments, and it has been very useful for the poets.

Such are the principal assertions that the occultists base upon the double authority of tradition and the direct vision of the Invisible Plane. We will now understand the response of a Brahmin, questioned by a Jesuit Father on the origin of his ideas on the transformations of the soul after death, and who responds to the brave missionary: "But, I have seen what is produced after death, and no revelation is equal to this certitude, especially if one performs the verification several times in order to get a clear idea of the details."

We may conclude here that which has reference to Human Magic, and we are going to speak now of Natural Magic, true metaphysics of the present Physics, and the one that many ancient Hermeticists studied in preference.

It had for its aim to have the concentrated human will act upon the living forces of Nature. Its key is: the *astral light*, acting in Nature as the astral body acts in man. The study of this genre of Magic is, in a great part, based upon *Astrology*, the planetary septenary and the zodiacal duodenary. All the magical operations are, indeed, subordinate to the astrological state of the heavens. This first point established, the operator strove to act upon the intelligences or "Spirits" of different orders which drive the various planes of nature. For the advanced occultist, all in nature is the work of Spirits of more or less elevated degrees. The classification of these Spirits plays a very great role in Natural Magic, thus it is necessary for us to insist a little upon this subject, so important and so obscure.

The *Spirits* are divided, for the occultists, into two principal large sections:

1. The Spirits inferior to human Nature, called by the ancients: Spirits of the elements, and by the moderns, since Parcelsus, *Elementals*. These Spirits are mortal but may acquire immortality by rising up to human nature.

It is to this category that are attached the Sylphs, or Spirits of the Air, the Salamanders, or Spirits of Fire, the Undines, or Spirits of Earth, and the Gnomes, or Spirits of the Earth, of the ancients and of the Rose-Croix. The Elementals act in Nature like embryonic cells act in man: they preside over the construction, destruction, and defense of the sections over which they have the guard.

Louis Michel de Figanières is the contemporary author who has best described them, under the name of "Humanimals" and Hominicules. It is these Spirits, themselves being neither good nor evil and acting well or badly according to the impulse which is given to them, which, in the spiritist séances, amuse themselves as Charlemagne or Victor Hugo, all at one price.

2. The second section is that of the Spirits equal or superior to Human Nature. It is here that it is necessary to classify the "planetary Spirits" of the Kabbalah and the Spirits of the deceased, called by certain modern occultists: Elementaries. It is necessary, furthermore, to have enter into this section the Spirits superior to man, those that the Church designates under the name of Angels and Demons, and a third category, known only by practitioners, and designated under the name of "Astral Spirits." It is these last that Valentinus designated under the terms of Pacific

What is Occultism?

Receivers, Receivers of the Archons, and even Archons in his *Pistis Sophia*. The Church wished to see here only demons, for it has lost all the keys of the astral plane. All these Spirits of the second section, having their own will, come at the time of the evocations and conjurations only if they are willing to do so, or if they have been forced there. One may force them only through conjuration, and if some detail of the ceremony is omitted, they have all power over the imprudent one who might have them obey without being worthy.

The magical ceremony has, therefore, a great importance, and we are going to summarize its principal phases. The preparation to the magical ceremony, or rather to the experience of Ceremonial Magic, consists in more or less prolonged fasts, and various physical and mental purifications. Furthermore, the operator and his aides (there must be an uneven number) ought to have prepared special vestments and a chamber of operation of the color corresponding to the chosen day. It is in this chamber that the magical circle is traced, formed by three concentric circles containing the divine names and the names of the Angels of the day and hour. The circle is the true fortress of the operator, for, as long as he remains enclosed within the circle, he is sheltered from the pernicious influences. Beyond the circle, the operator also possesses, as means of defense, a sword, and as means of command, a magic wand, the preparation of which requires a special ritual. In certain ceremonies which are attached more to the Goetia than to Magic, a victim and blood are made use of. Once entered into his circle, the operator begins aloud, the call to the Spirits: this call takes the name of *evocation* when the Spirit is humbly prayed, and of *conjuration* when one forces the Spirit through threats and Divine Names to manifest itself, even against its will. Once the apparition is obtained, it is indispensable to pronounce the dismissal of the influences which have presented themselves. It is only after the dismissal that the operator may leave the circle with impunity.

We have just summarized a general type of ceremonial magic. It is understood that this type is modified according to the rituals and the circumstances. But what is necessary above all to retain is that the occultists are forbidden strongly from ever evoking demoniacal Spirits, and that they even combat the sorcerers who give themselves to this practice. Moreover, Ceremonial Magic is generally forbidden, in the high fraternities where Theurgy is, with reason, greatly preferred to it. The rituals of Ceremonial Magic are most often as manuscripts. The Biblioteque Nationale possesses a very beautiful one entitled: "The Keys of Solomon." The Biblioteque de l'Arsenal possesses over all rituals of Sorcery. Among the printed books, the best is the adaptation of the Fourth Book of Agrippa by Pierre d'Aban. They have attempted modern translations, but they contain so many errors of meaning that it is best to have recourse to the originals. Another great variety of Ceremonial Magic was the practice of the Hermetic Great Work, following its course between the laboratory and the oratory. The colors of the Work reproduced the Mysteries of Creation, and the symbolic accounts of the ancient temples were, most often, but an adaptation. Moreover, one will find all the details on this point in the article Alchemy.

It remains for us to speak on Inversive Magic,

What is Occultism?

Black Magic or Sorcery. Stanislas de Guaita has defined it very well: *the putting into Work, for evil, the occult forces of nature.*

Whereas the Magist puts all his efforts into the evolution of the natural forces, the Sorcerer employs himself of all his forces to paralyze the free expansion of the evolutive forces to the benefit of the forces of death and involution. In the majority of cases, the one who believes himself endowed with a malefic power is a poor ignoramus who possesses only a puerile secret of magnetism, and who then utilizes to his best, his knowledge in order to terrorize his neighbors, and in order to extract their money. For it is still a characteristic distinction of the schools of occult initiation that it is absolutely forbidden to request or receive either gifts or money for one's personal needs in recompense for any assistance by magical means. It is thus that the talismans, which are generally simple fixers of magnetic forces, ought to be made personally by the one who wishes to utilize them, and should never be bought or sold, under pain of being banished by the serious schools of occultism. The Sorcerer who enters freely into struggle with all the divine forces of the invisible is, in the majority of the cases, a monomaniac of pride or alienated. It must not be believed that the lights projected everywhere by the science of the 19th century has made to disappear this type of grand revolt against God. One of the works of Stanislas de Guaita gives us a number of authentic documents on the Abbé Boullan, a defrocked priest calling himself a disciple of Vintras, and who had established at Lyon the seat of his operations. Now, an inquiry made on the former life of this so- called terrible sorcerer has revealed several condemnations, as much ecclesiastical and legal, which leaves no doubt as to the mental state of this would-be fiend of hell.

Magical charms, or action at a distance by means of an object in magnetic communication with the evil-doer, object called: Volt or Vult, has been very skillfully attached to deep Hypnosis and to the exteriorization of the senses by Mr. de Rochas, in a series of curious experiments. One of the more characteristic consists in having held far from the subject a piece of wax that they prick with a pin. The subject experiences the sensation of the prick as if they had done it to him directly. A photographic proof, from which the stereotype plate has been drawn into a state of exteriorization of the subject, presents analogous relations, even at a distance and without contact.

These experiments and others of the same kind have been verified by Dr. Luys and myself at the Charity: but they are too small in number to constitute anything other than indications, whose exact character the future will be charged with specifying.

The Pacts that the Sorcerer signed in his blood and remitted to the devil enter again into the category of conjurations and their cerebral consequences. It is the same of the Black Mass and other practices of the same type, which are attached to the Goetia.

The magic of the country-side with its simple formulas is not Sorcery, but rather, most often, of the mystical magnetism based on old Christian traditions. Thus, the formula to prevent burners from doing harm: Fire of God, lose your heat - As Judas lost his color - When he betrayed Our Lord - In the Garden of Olives - is a charm of the Elementals, like almost all the formulas employed in the country, and has nothing to do with the Goetia. On the contrary, to recite the "Pater" backwards in order to make milk turn, is a practice of Sorcery. For the Sabbat and other details, see *Sorcellerie*.

Theurgy acts only by means of the priest and the sacrifice. It is therefore the complete contrary of Magic, and we speak of it here because certain authors have cited it as the Divine Magic.

The theurgist, indeed, possesses the powers which constitute his quality only after having acquired some grace, whether through voluntary reincarnation or by any other cause of the same type. At his voice, and especially his prayer, Sickness and Death itself recoil and cease, human minds are modified and the astral stereotypes themselves may be changed or pushed back. These stereotypes are those that the prophets see form in the astral plane, and every prophecy may be thus annihilated by the action of a Theurgist. Such powers are not given to the prideful nor to the ambitious, and in order to avoid any diversion, the law wills that the Theurgist can do nothing, by mystical means, for himself or his own.

The physical plane being, for example, submitted to him, his children, if he is married to fully support all the social charges, otherwise his close relatives, are hostages to destiny. I know personally in France a human being endowed with such powers. I have seen, in the company of other medical colleagues, "mal de Pott" disappear in a few minutes, tibias become straight again, to speak only of medical feats. The healing is all the more powerful when the parents (when it is a question of children) or the petitioners have suffered more or have done more anonymous good around them. It is often forbidden to the

Theurgist to heal the child of a millionaire egotist, just as a poor street merchant will see his little one instantly snatched from Death.

Time and Distance do not exist, for the works of Theurgy, and the operator will see and act as well from Lyon to Paris as from one street to another. It is forbidden to name directly those who have such powers, and silence is what they seek above all. One will permit to conformity to this rule, all the more so as we have simply to differentiate here, Theurgy from Magic. Let us say in conclusion that Theurgy throws a bright light upon Christianity, and that the cult of Our Lord Jesus Christ, of the Virgin, and of the Saints, is inherent to these practices of High Theurgy, however ignored and dreaded by the Church which confuses Theurgists and Sorcerers into one same superstitious fear.

Few subjects present as many difficulties as the question of History, considered from the point of view of Occultism. In order to avoid, as best we can, the obscurities, we will divide our exposé into two principal parts:

1st, the history of the constitution of the various occult traditions;

2nd, the history of the influence exercised exteriorly in the profane world, by the various occult fraternities.

What is Occultism?

TRADITION

The Human Races and the Planetary Physiology
The Schisms of Irshou and the Shepherds
The Great Mysteries

In order to get a clear idea of the teachings of Occultism concerning the various traditions and their constitution, it is indispensable to make a preliminary digression on the human races and on planetary physiology, such as the occultists understand it.

We say physiology, for Esotericism teaches that each planet is a living being, and the Earth does not escape this general rule. The Earth, considered as an organism, has for organs the continents, as we will see shortly. Its circulation is constituted by the Ocean as heart, with an aerial arterial current of the Ocean to the mountains by the clouds, and to the valleys by the dew and the rain, a veinous current, returning by the rivers and streams.

Breathing is done, at the contact of the solar emanation by the cremation of the terrestrial atmosphere. Digestion is under the dependence of the terrestrial humus, immense stomach of absorption and transformation that man utilizes for his use in ameliorating. According to a very ancient tradition, confirmed by the revelations of Louis Michel de Figanières, the Earth is formed by the solder, the intimate union, of several planets on course for dissolution; each of these planets had constituted a terrestrial continent, and the nervous system, formed by networks and metallic veins, has gathered all under the direction of a unique

Spirit.

The most advanced planet was Asia, thus was it charged to instruct the others successively on the divine things. This mission ceased when terrestrial humanity was mature enough for the Christ to incarnate in Judea, at the meeting point of various terrestrial continents. One planet, after having accepted the incrustation with the others, refused to pursue the common evolution and was rejected alone with its advanced inhabitants, into the entourage of the Earth. This revolting planet is the Moon, and its abrupt disappearance was the cause of the inclination on the ecliptic and of an immense deluge. Each continent has therefore generated its flora and its fauna, as well as its special human race. Terrestrial humanity has, then, different points of departure, and does not come from a single source; it has brought equally personal traditions, and it is only later that these equally personal traditions have merged themselves into one another, at the same time that the men, the flora, and the fauna mingled through exchanges and commerce.

These notions may seem original or bizarre, but they are indispensible to know in order to understand a multitude of ideas of the ancients on Nature, and the modern occultists have preserved them integrally.

The races were four in number, differentiated by their origin and their color, and they had preponderance over the Planet in the following order:

1st, the Lemurians, natives of a continent which occupied the place of the present Pacific Ocean, and who would be a reddish yellow;

2nd, the Atlanteans, natives of a continent which was found at the place occupied today by the Atlantic

Ocean. They had red skin;

3rd, the Blacks, natives of present Africa;

4th, the Whites, natives of the environs of the North Pole (White Sea), and of the European continent, the last evolved.

For each continent, like each man, each family, and each nation has its periods of youth, maturity, and old age. Certain ones even have alternatives of sleep, burial under the water, and of awakening, separated by deluges that the Brahmins in their chronology, have set perfectly. Now, the occult tradition, presently in vogue among the whites, has forcibly submitted to the influence of all the preceding traditions, which obliges us to say a few words on each of these traditions, all derived from the single source to which the seers always refer.

On the Lemurian tradition, we possess only some odds and ends, preserved at Tibet and in some Taoist centers of China. This tradition, the nearest to the unity, was above all mathematical and strictly joined the number to the idea.

On the Atlantean tradition, we possess, on the contrary, much remaining. The Atlanteans had, indeed, all the coasts of the south of Europe; the Iberians, the Etruscans, and especially the Egyptians, are colonies of Atlantis. After the catastrophe which engulfed nearly all of the original continent, the colonies became centers of the greatest importance, for the later races. The Atlantean tradition, known especially by the hieroglyphs and monuments of primitive Egypt, studied the Absolute under all its forms.

The Black tradition is particularly attached to the study of the astral plane, under all its aspects; also the figures of demons, all the evocative ceremonies of astral Spirits, have their origin in this tradition.

Such are, very briefly summarized, the elements in the presence of which the white race is going to find itself, in the course of its various wanderings, that we are going to now give a summary of according to Fabre d'Olivet.

The cradle of the race was therefore placed around the White Sea, in the epoch when the blacks ruled over the planet and when they were installed in all the south of Europe and in the majority of the old red colonies, which they had subjugated by force, but from which they had adopted the arts and intellectuality.

This is even the reason for which the black race had such a rapid decline. Putting all its confidence in physical strength and military valor, it neglected its own intellectuality and the complete decadence followed its first defeats. The black explorers, hurled into adventure in the immense forests of the north, discovered the first specimens of the white race which had a bold point towards the south. We will not summarize the incessant struggle between the two races, which followed that discovery; and we will say simply that all was concluded to the profit of the whites who, in a few centuries had driven back the blacks to the south-east around the sea of the Blacks (present Black Sea) and into India which was still under the power of the Blacks. "There was a time," say the chronologies of the Brahmins, "when India was under the power of the Ethiopians."

It was in Europe the druidic epoch, 10,000 BC, and the continent was divided thus: to the east the land of the brutes, Ross-Land, cradle of the Race; advancing to the west and south, we find successively: the Raised Earth,

What is Occultism?

Poll-Land; the Divine Earth, Deutsch-Land; and the Limit of the Souls, Dabu-Mark; finally, we arrive at the Low Lands: Holl-Land and Goll-Land. It is at this moment that is placed the first exodus of the Whites towards the south. A large part of the Whites went around the Black Sea, gained Arabia, and constituted these men of firm resolution from whom eventually derived the Hebrew people.

Let us speak now of Ram.

Ram was a druid, to whom a dream revealed the manner to use the tincture of Mistletoe to heal leprosy, which threatened to completely destroy the white race. It is from here that dates the cult of the Mistetoe by the Druids. Having become, by his discovery, too popular, Ram was condemned to "go carry a message to the ancestors." That is to say to have his throat cut in a grand ceremony by the Druidesses, then very powerful. There was only one means to avoid this sad end: exile; and Ram was exiled, followed by several thousand Celts who attached themselves to his fortune. Ram first made for the Black Sea; then he went around it and established himself near the Ural Mountains, where he prepared, for several years, the execution of his grand project: the conquest of India over the Blacks.

When all was ready, he daringly hurled his Celts upon the Blacks, and in a few years these latter were pushed back unto the isle of Ceylon, where they were definitively crushed. According to the occultists, the historians who follow the descent of the Aryans of Asia into Europe begin their history only at this moment, and are unaware that the Aryans came to Europe only after having formerly come from there in order to conquer Asia.

Tradition

It is in the Brahmanic archives that the occultist historians have drawn this information that certain modern archaeological discoveries would tend to confirm, for the most part.

Ram constituted his tradition by uniting the cult of the ancestors with the red tradition and with the black tradition already implanted in India, and he changed his name from Ram, which meant Ram, into that of Lam, which signified Lamb. Lamaism came thus to be added to Brahmanism, in the constitution of the oriental tradition of the Whites.

We arrive now at the question, important for the ancients, of the Symbolism of the colors. This question has just been definitively resolved by one of the great seekers who has asked of Occultism the key of the ancient civilizations: Saint-Yves d'Alveydre, in his Chromatic Key of Symbolism. The Brahmins, representatives of the orthodox tradition, had, as symbol, the color white, that of the conquering race. Sanskrit reflects the true sacred writing (which, according to Saint-Yves, would be Watan) written from Occident to Orient (from left to right), in order to indicate the origin of the conquerors.

On the contrary, the Atlantean writings and their derivatives, are written from Orient to Occident (from right to left), while the writing of the Lemurians was traced from heaven to earth and from Orient to Occident (like present Chinese), and the writing of the blacks was written from earth to heaven. All corresponded strictly to all, in each tradition, and the manner of writing indicated analogically all the rest. The sacred color is also another precious guide. The orthodox Whites had the color white, we have said, when the first schism broke out, a schism at

What is Occultism?

once scientific, philosophical, and religious.

After thirty-five centuries of tranquility, this schism of Irschou broke out suddenly (around 3200 BC) and those who revolted left India, while taking the color red as their emblem, and seeking to combat the creations of the Orthodox, everywhere where those who revolted were stronger. They are called the Shepherds, Yonijas, to indicate their ignorance of the mysteries and their lack of intellectual references. The Shepherds left India, invaded Asia Minor, then Arabia, by driving back into the desert the old Celtic colonies. One of the waves of invasion went to found Tyre, from where purple, mark of the Shepherds across the world, became the symbol and the effective representation of the absolute Kings, dispensing with the authority of the tradition, Tyrants and Tyrians of every race that the initiates combatted everywhere with all their power. A torrent of these Shepherds, uniquely powerful through brutal force and scorn for the laws of civilization, invaded Egypt and seized the throne of the Pha-Ra-Ons (Dynasties of the Shepherds), while fortifying themselves on the side of India, in order to avoid a return of the Orthodox. To avoid the total loss of the ancient tradition, the orthodox priests of O-SIR-IS, in constant communication with the primitive centers, created the Great Mysteries which were going to play so considerable a role in the history of humanity. It is indeed from these Egyptian temples, having become around 2600 BC the central University of the Occident, that came the Revealers and Legislators charged with going to combat everywhere the disastrous work of the Tyrants.

These great men, who acquired Knowledge only after very firm physical, moral, and spiritual proofs, will radiate into all the Occident, and it suffices to cite Lycurgus, Solon, Numa, Minos, Pythagoras, and Plato on the one hand, then, Orpheus and Moses on the other, to see the importance of this central University, called Hermes, of which all the temples of the Occident were but secondary schools, in constant communication with the intellectual head which succeeded in erasing, by serving the Greeks as soldiers, the effects of the Shepherds and their descendants, against the orthodoxy.

It is necessary to understand the grandeur of the mission of Pythagoras, going through all the temples of India, and coming then to organize, at the Olympic Games, the resistance against the Persians who were preparing to invade the Occident; it is necessary to comprehend this mission, understood as the occultists understand it, in order to get a clear idea of the sacred respect which was attached, eventually, to this title of Pythagorean. The Greek philosophers were often only "...apes" of their masters, the Egyptians, to whom they wished to deny, later on, their intellectual paternity.

It is this struggle of initiation and the initiates against tyranny which constitutes, for the occultist, the esoteric key to history.

We will not leave this symbol of the colors without speaking of the attempt of the orthodox initiate who took the name of Fo-Hi to organize, around 2700 BC, the Far East civilization, with the color yellow as initiatic mark.

Chinese is the sole key, still existing, to what one may call an astral language, especially if we relate it to the ancient figurative characters Siang-Hin, which give the way of total reading of the hieroglyphs, Peruvian or Egyptian.

What is Occultism?

Let us leave now the general history in order to occupy ourselves with the constitution of the secret tradition of Moses, which is going to serve as basis to all orthodoxy in the Occident, until the arrival of Jesus.
Moses created for the Occident what Fo-Hi had created for the Orient: a People charged to carry across the ages, a symbolic and initiatic summary of the whole of ancient Occultism; a holy ark, a Thebah (א ב ת) contained under some hieroglyphic characters what, later on, Daniel revealed to Esdras under the form of the present square Hebrew. But, according to Saint-Yves d'Alveydre, Moses wrote in Watan characters.

The work entrusted by Moses to his initiates contained the synthesis of the knowledge of the Reds, acquired by Moses in Egypt, as a priest of Osiris, and the knowledge of the Blacks, acquired in the service of his father-in-law Jethro, in the temple of the desert. These two traditions had been, furthermore, strictly verified in the secret light of nature through ecstasy and direct vision, which had unified the revelation and had brought back to the real point of view the ancient chronicles of Ioah, by which Moses was inspired. The intellectual creator of the Hebrews constituted his book in Spirit, Soul, and Body, as an organism which it was, and in the following fashion: the Body was the Massora, or rules for writing or copying the sacred characters, with prohibitions from changing any of it, under pain of spiritual death. The Soul, double and infinitely expansive like all souls, was the Talmud, or judicial code, with its two poles: the Mishma and the Ghemarah. Finally, the Spirit of the work that, alone, Moses transmitted in his lifetime orally, was the Kabbalah.

Tradition

It is to this Kabbalah, transmitted more or less faithfully up to the moment when Saint John revealed it in his *Gospel* and his *Apocalypse*, that is referred the majority of the initiatic societies of the Occident devoted to the defense of Christ, whereas it is to Pythagoreanism that the current pagan is referred.

To summarize the teachings of the Kabbalah would be to reproduce the entire theoretical section of this article, with Hebraic terms. We shall return, then, to our historical exposé. The white tradition is thus constituted with its particular character, since Moses. But there exists another traditional current, with a character more political, moreover, than intellectual: it is the Pythagorean current, to which will be attached many political secret societies pursuing the destruction of personal power, and this leads us to our second section:

What is Occultism?

INFLUENCES OF THE OCCULT SOCIETIES

In the Profane World

Let us cast a glance to the past and imagine that ancient civilization called pagan, asking ourselves: What are its secret means?

It is those Fraternities of Initiates, come out of the local temples or from the central University of Egypt, and whose members circulated from temple to temple without having need of money, thanks to the law of hospitality and to the signs of recognition which open all the doors upon the entire Earth; for these so-called pagans knew not the wars of religion, and knew how to make of the temple of the different astral or divine forces, a sanctuary of the sole Truth. Plato, made a slave, will owe to the secret signs of the initiates his immediate liberation. What was necessary, then, to be part of one of these Fraternities? Money? No, for all was free of charge, and the pupil was lodged and fed freely during all his studies. Was it necessary to be a patrician and of high birth? No, for initiation was open to all, slave or not, and one sole thing was required: a physical courage at every trial, an absolute contempt of Death, necessary pledges for the missions which, later, could be entrusted to the initiate. After the trials, the initiation began, and rose with difficulty even as the trials progressively elevated to the moral plane, then to the spiritual plane.

Homer, Virgil, have described, under the name of

descent into the underworld, the various phases of these initiations which constituted, in antiquity, the class all the more truly ruling that its members were disinterested and occult. It is by this light of the initiations, say the occultists, that it is necessary to take up and reconstitute the whole history of antiquity.

The great change occurring in the regimen of the initiations was not due to the persecutions, however numerous, that the known centers suffered on the part of the Tyrants, but to the birth of Christianity. The Magi, representatives of Chaldean initiation, which had already given back to Esdras the lost keys, came to bow to the cradle of the Religion of the Occident, and we see the four forms of the sphinx characterizing each one of the evangelists of the Divine Word. At the same time, the oracles keep silent, which indicates that the pass-word, come from the invisible centers, was indeed to give all possible support to this Christianity which, alone, was going to make the first cut into the struggle against the Roman Tyrany which pursued with tenacity the destruction of all the sanctuaries of High Initiation. Thus do we see, under the name of Gnostics, the initiates of all the centers giving a considerable support to the nascent Christianity. Saint Paul will be the practical Realizer of the new organism, but Saint John the Evangelist and author of the Apocalypse, will ever remain the Initiate.

At this moment, all the centers walk in accord in favor of the Christian revelation, and the struggle is pursued until the surrender of Christianity to the Roman administration, by bishops preferring the temporal to the spiritual. Starting from this moment, the persecutions against the centers of initiation resumed worse than ever,

What is Occultism?

but they are directed, this time, by the members of the Christian clergy who, under the pretext of heresy, wished to annihilate every trace of the ancient tradition. It is in this way that began the incessant struggle between the free idea and Constantinople; then, after the taking of this city, in the Universities of the Arabs, so tolerant, these mysterious associations of Hermeticists, initiated Knights, Adepts of Saint John, etc. All these forms were grouped during the middle ages, first in Westphalia, starting from the year 772, under the name of Free-Counts or Free-Judges, then in all of Europe and part of Asia, starting from 1186, by the Templars.

The Templars were on the verge of reconstituting the ancient Fraternity of the ancient temples, with its signs of recognition and its agents spread out everywhere; they had prepared themselves to endow Christendom with a broad and diffused instruction, which would have made humanity advance several centuries, when, in 1312, they were betrayed and soon dispersed. The survivors of the massacre, understanding that their error had been to abandon the way of the ancient initiatic Fraternities, were mirrored in relation to the representatives of the Pythagorean initiation, then existing, and laid down the basis of those associations of Illuminati from where eventually came the majority of the Masonic rites.

It is in connection with the various Secret Societies that one will find details that we are obliged to summarize, so as not to go beyond the limits of our subject, and we are now going to see how, abandoning the path of material struggles, the Initiates are going to call the Idea alone to the service of their cause by disguising their preoccupations under the veil of alchemical research and

Philosophy.

Occultism & Philosophy

It does not suffice to assert the influence of Occultism upon Philosophy, it is necessary above all to prove this influence by dates and names. We are going, then, to give an enumeration of the principles among the philosophers that the occultists considered as being of their own, and we will recall simply that we recognize the Initiates and Disciples of the esoteric tradition by their trinitary doctrine and by the admission of an intermediary plane of beings between the physical and the divine (astral plane of Paracelsus and of the Martinists). There exist, as we have said, two principal currents in the occidental tradition:

1st, the Pythagorean and Platonic current, formed of very erudite men and scholars, but generally opposed to Christian mysticism and with rather pagan tendencies (for the moderns);

2nd, the Christian current, which contains nearly all the Encyclopedists of Occultism and its greatest Realizers. We are obliged to made an enumeration, perhaps monotonous, but which will help the bibliographical research to such a degree, that we have been unable to dispense with it.

Pythagorean & Platonic Current

What is Occultism?

In the original Pythagorean School, derived directly from Egypt and from the Atlantean tradition, we cite: Pythagoras, Charondas, Lysis, Aristeus, Alcmeon, Timeus of Locres, Œnopide, Archytas of Taranto, Philolaus, Stesimbrote of Thasos.

In the Academy, it is necessary above all to remember the names of Plato, Speusippeus, Phormion, Crates, of an initiate: Axioteus, and especially Xenocrates, who attempted to establish the connections of Platonism with Pythagoreanism, by reducing the ideas to the corresponding numbers. It is the same idea that Will be taken up again in the first century BC by Antiochus of Ascalon.

We will not especially cite Aristotle, because, although initiated, he has developed through writing only the exoteric, and has kept the esoteric for the oral teaching of rare disciples, among others, Alexander the Great. His apologists, being unaware of the existence of the esotericism, have transformed Aristotle to such a degree that we will not consider any member of the Lycée as a true initiate.

So, let us pass immediately to the Neo-Pythagoreanism of the 1st century with Euxene of Heracleus and especially his illustrious disciple: Apollonius of Tyana and his successors, Anaxilas of Larisse, Moderatus, Nicomachus of Gerassa (2nd century) and the initiator of Cato: Nearchus. We place beyond comparison the illustrious Apulius, one of the last initiates of the great mysteries, and one of the rare revealers of esotericism.

Let us come to the Neoplatonists, those who give the most light on the astral plane and the astral Spirits, among whom we will remember: Areius Didymus (under the reign of Augustus), Thrasylle (under the reign of Tiberius, who had him killed), Plutarch, disciple of Ammonius of Alexandria, and who revealed under jocular appearances rather profound truths, in his treatise on Isis and Osiris. Albinus, one of the initiators of Galien, Maximus of Tyre, Taurus Caluisius, who counted Aulu-Gelle among his audience, Ptolemy of Alexandria, and, not to forget the female initiates: Arria.

From the School of Alexandria, we must cite all. After Numesius of Apanée, we will pause especially upon the name of one of the greatest among the initiates: Ammonius Saccas. Ammonius is to be considered as having endowed Christianity with its whole ritual, the principle of which is drawn from Mazdaism, but he has given rise to such a pleiad of brilliant pupils, that humanity ought to remember his name. Among these pupils, we cite, after Herenius and Origen, the inspirer of Allan Kardec, good in spite of himself, Plotinus, who, in his turn, gave rise to two great traditional currents: and occidental current, confided to Porphyry, and an oriental current, confided to Amelius, who developed above all the mystical practice. Porphyry had for his successor, at the head of the school, the illustrious Iamblicus, who was succeeded in the 4th century by Adesius, himself followed, at the head of the school founded in Cappadocia, by Eustathius.

Let us return to the foundation at Athens of a new School by Plutarch of Athens (356-436), who initiated his daughter Asclepigenia, herself an initiator, with Syrianus, pupil of Proclus, and let let us conclude what concerns this illustrious School which attempted to diffuse the mysteries, by recalling the names of Hierocles, Hypatia, to whom the initiation was fatal, and Olympiodore and Damascius, remembering also the renowned of the school in the 5th and 6th centuries. We pass over the purely alchemical current, to arrive in 1400 where we will find to cite Nicolas de Cusa (1401-1464), Marsile Ficin (1433-1499), the master of Pico de la Mirandola, Patricius Patrizzi (1526-1567) and Giordano Bruno (1548-1601), the inspirer of Descartes, Spinoza, Leibnitz, Schelling, and also Hegel.

Spinoza (1632-1677) opens the series of philosophers being inspired by the Jewish Kabbalah, in its non-mystical section, and his disciples Cuper, Cufaeler, Parker, Law, and Wachter pursued, more or less successfully, the same path.

The more modern representatives of this Pythagorean current are: Hamann (1730-1788), Baader, Statler, Frederick Shlegel, and Weishaupt, realizer of the society of the "Illuminati" and who lived from 1748 to 1830.

We will conclude this list by the name of the angel of this current of erudition and philosophy, that we name Fabre d'Olivet, one of the most scholarly men that Occultism has produced.

Mystical & Christian Current

It is in this current that we are going to recount the true Masters of contemporary Occultism, and its most illustrious representatives, whether ancient or modern. Thus will we insist only upon the most important from among them.

There are, of course, the Gnostics, who open the

series, and it is by them that we are to begin our citations. Simon Magus, Cerinthius, and especially Saturninus, one of the Kabbalists of the Gnosis, then Bardaisan, Basilides, and finally Valentinus, the author of the Pistis Sophia, and the head of the Gnostic school of Alexandria, Carpocrates, very esteemed by the occultists, Marcion and Manes for the battalion of Christians striving to unite Faith to Phiolosphy and Science. Among the members of the Church, the occultists claim Saint John and Saint Paul as being of their own.

This latter is the one who has most contributed to the diffusion of the trinitary constitution of man in "Spiritus, Anima, and Corpus."

To recover the continuation of the Christian occult current, we will skip to Tauler (1290-1361), Eckart (1260-1328), founder of mysticism in Germany, and his pupil Suso (1300-1365), creator of the Fraternity of the "Friends of God." These are all adversaries of Scholasticism, that pagan creation of Aristotle, under the color of Christian orthodoxy. Thus all the initiates, whether instructed orally like Gerson (1362-1429), the firm defender of the trinitary doctrine of the three spheres of Man, or Petrarch, or whether illumined by the direct Vision, like Ruysbrœk, called the Admirable, have been the adversaries of Scholasticism, as well as the cultured and the reformers like Ange Pollien (1454-1494), Rudolph Agricola (1444-1480) and Luther.

We arrive now at the Encyclopedists and the Realizers of Occultism, the only ones who are considered without debate as mystics by the critics and historians. Let us cite, by approximate order of dates, Reuchlin (1455-1522), Johannes Pico de la Mirandola (1463-1494), and his

What is Occultism?

son Francis, Cornelius Agrippa, counsel of Charles the Fifth and author of the Occult Philosophy, the first real encyclopedia of the matter. Agrippa lived from 1486 to 1535.

Ricci, Leon the Hebrew, and especially Paracelsus (1493-1541), the great realizer and grand master of Scientific Occultism, the creator of Homeopathy, and the one who has best studied the Astral Plane and Astral Body to which he has given their name.

Cardan (1501-1576), the most humble and scholarly of the Illuminati, Guillaume Postel, the Resurrected (1510-1581), Bayer, Mennens, and Valentine Weigel, pupil of Tauler and Paracelsus, complete this list which is continued with: Jacob Bœhme (1575-1624), the inspirer and guide of nearly all the Illuminati, Robert Fludd (1574-1637), encyclopedist and realizer and founder, by order of the Rose-Croix, of Freemasonry, Pordage (1625-1698), teacher, first, then pupil of Jeanne Leade, and finally, Von Helmont the Father (1577-1644), the Paracelsus of the 17th century, and his son, Francis Von Helmont (1618-1699), who exercised such a great influence over Goethe and Leibnitz, who, furthermore, aided in the publication of the "Kabbala Denudata" and Angelius Silezius (1624-1677) and Poir (1646-1719), leads us to Swedenborg (1688-1777).

Swedenborg is known above all as a philosopher and seer, but that does not bear in mind his work of realization, which is, however, more grandiose. It is to Swedenborg that are attached, indeed, all the truly Christian Fraternities of the Occident, for he was the master of Martinès de Pasqually (1715-1779) who, himself, initiated Claude de Saint-Martin (1743-1803). Lavater

Influences of the Occult Societies

(1741-1801), who may be considered as one of the precursors of Spiritism, de Maistre (1753-1821), de Bonald (1753-1840), and Ballanche (1776-1847) lead us to Wronski and Eliphas Lévi (the Abbé Constant), to whom, with Louis Lucas, are attached nearly all the contemporary occultists.

But before passing to the present era, we must return again to the past in order to recall the names of several occultists who have not been able to find a place in the preceding enumeration, reserved especially to the philosophers.

We will recall, then, the astrologer d'Ailly, Albertus Magnus, bishop of Ratisbonne and teacher of Saint Thomas, to whom is attributed a Grimoire which has nothing to do with sorcery. Abumazar, astrologer of the 9th century, Apomazar, celebrated Arab soothsayer; Pierre d'Apone, known as a magician (1270), the Marquis d'Argens, born in 1704 in Provence, and author of the *Lettres Cabalistiques*; Armide, made famous by Tasso, Arnauld de Villeneuve, alchemist and astrologer, Roger Bacon, Basile Valentine, Jean Bodin, Henri Boguet, Balthazar Bakker, who had occupied himself with the occult from the judicial point of view, Barri, alchemist of the queen Christine, Thomas Bungey, and let us not forget Cagliostro, charged with his mission by the Illuminati of Germany, and considered as a charlatan by the profane. Cagliostro, endowed with rather extensive magnetic and necromantic knowledge, laid the practical bases of the Revolution, which he had come to organize. Let us cite, then, in alphabetical order, Dom Calmet, the author of the Dissertation on "Revenants and Vampires," Thomas Campanella, Catherine de Medici and Charles of England were occupied, the first with sorcery, the second with alchemy.

Bartholomew Cocles, the famous chiromancer of the 16th century, the demonographer Pierre Delancre, the Jesuit Delrio, author of "Magical Research," Didymus the possessed, the German seer Engelprecht, died in 1642, the famous Etteila, from his true name Aliette, the renovator of Cartomancy, the Abbé Faria who discovered verbal suggestion, the seer of the 16th century, Falgenhaver, the alchemist Fioraventi, author of the "Treasure of Human Life" (1570), Nicolas Flamel, who, according to oral tradition, would still be living in Asia Minor, and was one of the most elevated adepts, the great Kabbalist Jacques Gaffarel, Garinet, author of *l'Histoire de la Magie en France*, Gaufridi, a poor lunatic whom they burned as a sorcerer in 1611; the astrologer Luc Gauric born in 1476, and in whom Catherin de Medici had great confidence, and Urbain Grandier, that unwitting sorcerer, executed on the deposition of some hystericals. A pope, Gregory VII, figures among the writers on Occultism, the Spanish magician Grillandus, the alchemist Gustenhover, the two Isaacs of Holland, Jehan de Meung, the author of *Roman de la Rose*, that Dante completed by the *Roman de la Croix*, and Saint-Jerome himself, are considered as occultists in the list of Ferdinand Denis. A special mention is due to Athanasius Kircher, Jesuit who had the ability to have his works printed by the Vatican; under the pretext of attacking Occultism, he made thereof a very complete encyclopedic exposé. Kircher is known by the invention of the magic-lantern; he died at Rome in 1680.

After him we cite the popular astrologer Mathieu Laensberg, then Langlet Dufresnoy, author of the History of Hermetic Philosophy, classic still today in the schools of occultism. The Marquis Le Gendre, author of the Treatise of the Opinion, the demonographer Pierre Le Loyer, the bard Merlin, of the 5th century, the chiromancer Moreau that Napoléon consulted, Gabriel Naudé and Nostrodamus, the most celebrated of the prophets, contemporary and ancient. Among those that we have not yet cited, are found also: Gilles de Retz, a lunatic who gave rise to the legend of Blue Beard, and who was burned alive in 1440, Cosma Ruggieri, another astrologer of Catherine de Medici, Raymond Lulle, considered deservedly as one of the Grandmasters of Hermeticism, the Comte de Saint-Germain, collective name of the Illuminati who confided to Cagliostro his mission, the sorcerer Trois-Echelles, burned under Charles IX, the Abbé de Villars, assassinated for having revealed certain practices of the Rose-Croix (he was killed on the road from Lyon in 1673) and, to close this list, the pupil of Agrippa, Jean Wierus, who published important studies on demonology. We see, by all those names, the importance acquired by Occultism in every era and its action upon the most elevated minds. There would have to be a special section dedicated to the influence of the Occult Science on literature.

When we recall that Shakespeare was initiated, that Goethe practiced Hermeticism, and that, nearer to us, Balzac was a Martinist and that Edgar Allen Poe was affiliated with Pythagorean groups, we will have indicated the great lines of this influence.

What is Occultism?

CONCLUSION

We have had to lay out the philosophy of occultism as broadly as our framework has permitted us. We have made our efforts to give at least a brief overview of all these theories on the astral, on the plastic mediator, and on the evolution of the Spirit, that many critics know only by the deformations that the authors of the classical treatises and encyclopedias have made thereof. But we must not lose sight that the ideas that we have perhaps badly summarized have given rise to very great developments, that the avid seeker of certain notions ought to consult in preference to this too hasty a study.

We will also note that we have done our best not to sacrifice to the ideas of the day.

We do not conceal form ourselves, indeed, the astonishment that the exposés on the Earth considered as a living being, on Christ and the Redemption, on the mystical faculties of the human being, and on prayer, are going to cause to the critics imbued with the contemporary scientific ideas, if they condescend to throw a glance upon these pages.

We have ourselves traversed the various stages of this intellectual evolution which leads from atheistic materialism to philosophical pantheism, and from there to rational Christianity, disentangled form all the algae and clerical moss.

Our conviction is all the more firm thereby. They will have the goodwill to invent new words, or to deny the most evident psychic feats, they will be obliged, in the last resort, to return therefrom to the theories of Occultism

Conclusion

and to its methods in order to clearly and rationally explain the phenomena of telepathy, prophetic vision, psychic action at a distance, and exteriorization, which will become more and more certain, and more and more numerous eventually.

Thus do we hope that aside from the violent critiques that the preceding pages will not fail to provoke, there will be found perhaps some souls who will discover here the path which leads to the only ideal that we may seek on Earth: THE PEACE OF THE HEART through the scientific certitude of survival and by the comprehension of the justice of the Word in all the planes.

Such is our hope…

ENDNOTES

1. *Precis de physiologie synthétique*, by Doctor Encausse.
2. See: *La Réincarnation* by Papus.
3. See: *Précis philosophie synthétique* and *Comment est constitué l'être humain* by Papus.
4. *La Cabbale* (Papus)
5. *Tarot des Bohémiens. - Tarot divinatoire* by Papus.
6. *La Reincarnation* (Papus).
7. In natural theology, the part of metaphysics which treats God and his attributes.
8. See: *La Cabbale* (Papus).
9. See: *Ce que deviennent nos morts*, by Papus.

www.ingramcontent.com/pod-product-compliance
Lightning Source LLC
Chambersburg PA
CBHW020949090426
42736CB00010B/1341